MADONNA, COMPLEX

Madonna, Complex

Jen Stewart Fueston

CASCADE *Books* • Eugene, Oregon

MADONNA, COMPLEX

The Poiema Poetry Series

Cascade Books
An Imprint of Wipf and Stock Publishers
199 W. 8th Ave., Suite 3
Eugene, OR 97401

www.wipfandstock.com

PAPERBACK ISBN: 978-1-7252-6080-1
HARDCOVER ISBN: 978-1-7252-6081-8
EBOOK ISBN: 978-1-7252-6082-5

Cataloguing-in-Publication data:

Names: Fueston, Jen Stewart, author.

Title: Madonna, complex / Jen Stewart Fueston.

Description: Eugene, OR: Cascade Books, 2020 | Series: Poiema Poetry Series | Includes bibliographical references.

Identifiers: ISBN 978-1-7252-6080-1 (paperback) | ISBN 978-1-7252-6081-8 (hardcover) | ISBN 978-1-7252-6082-5 (ebook)

Classification: PS3556.U4 M3 2020 (print) | PS3556.U4 (ebook)

Manufactured in the U.S.A.   APRIL 8, 2020

for my family & friends

" . . . a prayer the body makes entirely."

—Seamus Heaney, *St. Kevin & the Blackbird*

"The kingdom does come. For me, this is how"

—Katie Ford, *Address I*

Contents

Contents

Contents

Dualism for Beginners

We don't choose what we believe in. Toddlers sing-song
you can't see me, you can't see me, even though
they've only closed their eyes. You know the soul
by how it wakes inside you when you're looking

in a mirror and you see yourself see you. This strange
unrecognition felt before you learn the difference
between mind and brain, that science can't locate
the part of us that knows its knowing. There must be days

this first makes sense, but girls feel out such riddles
with their hands. Right there in chapter one, this earth
we think we're other than takes form, and we're an urge
of breath blown through the dust. The way a child plucks

dandelions and blows the star-shaped seeds through air.
They don't know they're made of earth until they fall.

I.

Jeanne D'Arc

Et toi, que réponds tu à l'amour?

As with Mary, it was
the sound of angel wings
that broke the silence.
My ears rang gold. I felt fire
sprouting from
the dun earth.

Light spilt over the green valley—
on my head a warmth
settled, and began to spread.
I heard the sound of beating pulses
between bird-notes, heard the sound
water makes falling from a clay pitcher,
felt my blood running warm in my veins,

and then he came.
Do not ask why God
sometimes whispers his wisdom
to women too young to keep secrets.

This slow coming alive, a burning,
God, a flaming-red coal
in my throat. I heard him
come and settle in the fields of France,
heard him ask,

With what will you answer my love?

Tekakwitha

I asked the poem to give me its form
and it gave me a ladder climbing
into air and disappearing.

I listened for voices
and it showed me instead
the irrational shapes of desire,

how they look like doorways
opening into darkness
but also like votives

lit at the feet of a saint
whose name in native tongue means
she-who-bumps-into-things

she wasn't looking for,
she who wears her wounding
like a charm,

she who stumbles
in the formless air
and calls it holy.

Bird Psalm, Morning

A morning choir of gulls tip throats
open to gulp thin-bright air. Bodies
bone-vases of sound. They call
one square to life, depart, and
round the distant chimneys,
rousing those.

Terns weave little webs by wings,
pull rays through pinking air,
ribbon slow as the crimson flags,
brindle the sky with wings and songs.

No prayer-call stirs them first,
they dazzle the city, waking light,
wheeling shadows over stucco walls,
over child and veiled mother,
over old palaces of kings,
over fishermen and eager waiters,

over the teacher on her balcony.
The birds pray as I wish to,
wings out, with a graceful falling.

Saturday (1)

The world stills.
A tree, empty,
rounds its arms in
the open blue-dome,
a vigil-posed
oaken globe.

The world stills.
A caught breath,
as all woods and waves,
warbles, trills
call. And silence
answers.

The world stills. The
old air—empty—
while earth,
the tomb,
ripens.

Perestroika

The amphitheater smells of dank chlorine and tired
Soviet bricks. Late autumn sun lilts down
on briny water churning in a dingy pool.

Dolphins lift off the water's surface, curve gray bodies
through hoops, over arcs of spray, jump in time
to strains of Elvis or the "Beach Boys' Greatest Hits."

We laugh and clap along to music. Ira rolls her eyes
tells me, every year for fifteen now, this show remains
the same. And still, we are transfixed, open-mouthed,

by beleaguered creatures leaping from concrete pools.
Nothing dims it. It's a cool September Sunday,
on the far side of an old map's iron borders,

trainers pose on backs of dolphins, and I imagine
New Jerusalem, new heavens and new earth.
All those lions lying down with lambs.

On Being Asked if I Share the Gospel with My Students

I know I'm not getting any of this guy's money.
Because this is the missionary equation—
I with my presentation and my worn out
shoes, a life honed to a single point.

He with the presumption that he's sending me,
like a spy or a timebomb, into the forsaken
darkness, like a single ember bright-lit
in a censer swung across the map.

His is a gospel of nets, of capture. His is the gospel
that asks, *If you died tonight, do you know for sure
you'd go to heaven?* A gospel of the escape
route, the secret doorway, the cheat.

I can speak his language like a native, but can't
quite find a way to tell him: I am no ember.
That mine is a gospel of tanks
rusting in the snow, a gospel of grass

growing over the place they massacred
their neighbors, a gospel of guard shacks peeling
off their paint, gospel of old songs being sung
in the tavern, of year by year clear water filling up

the empty missile silo, of new bricks
making straight the rough streets.

Bird Psalm, Evening

Here at this table,
in the evening light,
Bach in my head and ears
and blood,

I am jealous of one white gull
carving the sky with out-stretched wings.
Jealous of pigeons nestling by twos
on chimney-stacks of tiled roofs—

I am even jealous of the bee
pacing up and down the pane,
its paper wings
lifting it toward the wall of light.

They all soar up into
great blue light,
They can praise God
with their feet
                off the ground.

All Saints Day, Istanbul

Morning in pajamas
speaking of the saints—
how their questions
could not have been
heavier than ours,

I think of Saint Teresa,
splayed in transfiguration.
Julian trembling in her cell.
Saint Francis stumbling hillsides
letting birds go free.
Saint Lucia blinded
by numinous light.

The prayer call rends
the rain-soaked air—
so we bend our necks,
cup hands. Try to
catch what it is
they must have known.

Detail of a Peacock

Nestling in the niche between the chapel's crumbling
arches, his long blue neck plucks nibbles of tessera.

He wanders through mosaic parables like something risen
out of time, wearing fashion all wrong for Byzantium—

a jaunty tri-plume hat in an age of halos. You presume
at first this must have been a gold-leaf sermon contra

vanity, or like those tapestry-arrested unicorns, an
attempt to tame our lusts of flesh. His sumptuous blue

feathers with their knowing eyes seem destined
for a harem girl's accessory, so what are they doing here?

What Augustine wrote at Carthage, though, unveils
the peacock's changing reputation, that before

its current turn as vain pretender, or the empty suit,
the Church discovered peacock flesh does not decay.

So poke at any early Christian tomb and there
they preen, depictions of life that does not die, the

incorruption of brief bodies made eternal. How every
year a feather's molt returns brighter and more beautiful.

This long-necked fellow settles into tessellation,
his plumage not quite all unfurled

so not to draw too much attention, but whispers that
he's hiding here for now, a creature caught

in colored bits of glass, waiting till these ruins
are restored to make his move.

At Hagia Irene

This is the place they made the creeds.
Which I suppose is like the place
they split the atom. Light from light,
true God from true God,
hydrogen and helium
both begotten, not made.

I feel like there should be a crater
in this old Byzantine clay,
but there are only pigeons
roosting in the bougainvillea. A trio
of grey wings among the leaves,
dusty and mottled until they split the sun,
are iridescent underneath the dust.

There's a reason they called the test sites Trinity,
a fission of wholenesses, a dazzling darkness as
attempts to dissect mystery result in fire and
annihilation. Try to peer at all things
visible and invisible and nature cleaves
like a Godhead made both of matter
and of flame. This is the place they split
the atom. Which I suppose is like
the place they made the creeds.

I envy the pigeons chattering
in the eaves of Saint Irene,
that they can nest in cool tiled hallways
dark-bright from the sunlight off the sea,
how they don't try to outwit the matter
that holds them, how they've learned
to live at angles to the light
that scatters off their wings.

Renunciation

Could Mary have refused,
when it was offered her,
left her fingers
open around the gift,
releasing the weight of it
from the palm of her hand?

Could she simply have turned
when the angel startled her,
and gone about folding the clothes,
sweeping dust from corners,
baking the daily bread?

Could she have brushed it aside,
arm upraised not in fear
but release?
A wave of good-bye,
a hand blocking merely the glare
of the morning sun,
not the radiance of angels
in her kitchen.

The Virgin, Home from the Mall

Dante Gabriel Rossetti's is my favorite—
an annunciation to the sullen, Mary

thin and limp-haired, slumped against the white-
washed wall, imaginary shopping bags strewn

carelessly at her feet. Her lips are rose, precisely lined.
She stopped off at Sephora for this shade, *thornberry*.

She likes the way it stains her mouth as if it's pricked, like
Sleeping Beauty's finger on the spindle. She's fairy-tale,

half-asleep, a slip of skin so translucent she's invisible,
the way young mothers are invisible, receptacles for bread

or salt, laundry or children, history or soap—emptied
of everything but light. In her earbuds (hidden by that

yellow halo) voices *whisper words of wisdom, let it be.* Only now
she notices, this stranger's feet are flame. He's suspended

in the air beside her bed, a dream settling like cloth. Before
the moment of enveloping, there's pause between the utterance

and acceptance. She bends, a heavy blossom. Her body
a parentheses, she curves away from glory, like we all do.

Saturday (2)

Christ as the seed in
the belly of earth.
Christ, the dung and dirt
beneath.
Christ, the bulb that's
dormant-lying.
Christ as the husk of flesh
dug deep.

Christ, the fallow
field awaiting.
Christ, the wing
still thick-cocooned.
Christ as the pearl
in field hiding.
Christ, the long-awaited bloom.

Christ, the round-egg
not yet woken.
Christ, the tongue's word
half-formed, half-spoken.

II.

Ash Wednesday

The point of fasting is
to fail. To learn your body

is more ass than angel.
That you cannot think

your way to God. But if
you're fortunate you might

crawl there, ashen, mucky,
knee-bent, bowed, in

the body you were born in.
The skin and sinew that will turn

to mineral and matter. Don't
forget. No matter, try to tame it,

make it mind you. As if you were
its keeper, not its ghost.

Istanbul Cafe, Rainstorm

We're caught in the city of longings,
in press and pulse of flesh.

Boats below plow
in rippling wakes, carve
through the Golden Horn.

Draped women cluster in groves,
lost under curtains of black.

People everywhere
steam like dragons,
hot breath warming the marble room.

Terrace chairs tilt toward tables,
kneeling before sleep.

One crystal lamp spatters light
in soft feathers
over the green cushions.

Faces seem cut and polished
as chandelier prisms,

shaped for the catching of light.

On Galata Bridge

The body knows itself
in time suspended,
silver-skinned fish
hooked from the sea.
Light catches as we are caught
and reeled,
held taut in the sweetening air.

Purity Culture

We were taught not
to throw ourselves
away, our bodies
the soft petals of white
flowers picked off
one by one, or soiled
like sheets. No one wants
to unwrap a gift that has
already been opened,
they said, which just means
we were still meant to be
given. Which just meant,
men and gods both
thought they deserved
offerings. But
innocence is tricky
to attain. It only is
until it isn't, a prize made
out of nothingness. And
purity is only ever lost.

Bodies of Water

I remember the sun taut on your back
before we dove in, and the junipers
on the hill around the cove. You set
your glasses on the concrete pier
beside your shirt. I remember waiting
til you were far out from the dock
before stripping to my underwear and
jumping into salt and brackish blue.

When I was young there was a game
we played at slumber parties. Laughing
in our nighties we made each other say
the way it felt to swim. We named
sensations: weightless, calm, electric,
free—think, even now can you explain
how the body can be left behind
in water? Can you describe belief
in being held? This, we'd giggle wide-eyed,
innocent, is how you'll feel when you have sex.

Nearly every afternoon I'd swim
two dozen laps trying to outdistance you.
Sometimes there beside me, sometimes
imaginary, always pulling against water
until my arms were dripping with resolve.

Every day, the water held me the way
I would let no one else. At night,
I looked out on the strait, lights pooling
in the current, freighters plodding through
the passageway, ferries coughing from
their yellow smokestacks, fishing dinghies
pulling silver bodies from the seam—
everything alive and pulsing on the swells.

We'd drink *raki* on the balcony, eating apricots
while the final prayer calls hollowed out the sky.
You didn't believe in the soul, the way I didn't
believe in the body. I thought that'd be enough
to keep me. That it might be enough for us both.

Bosporus Strait

The day as ripe
as apricots,
as sweet.

Tongue reaches out
to savor the soft
invite of air.

Body turns and
turns on
unmarred sheets.

In the seam
between us waterways—
continents—bleed.

To the Guest Who Broke a Wine Glass at My Party

Why is the neck of a wine glass slender,
unless for snapping clean?
The fecund rose bush chokes the fence.
Sun-bruised apples fall in faded grass.
A strung-bulb splinters on the bricks, and
spills its measured light in breeze-bent trees.
What's a garden for but feasting, or
a throat for ruining with praise?

But the broken morning's scattershot
with half-full cups and reckoning.
We second-guess our sweetest messes. Yet,
what use a heart that's never wrecked by joy?
Clear droplets gleam in grass and
it doesn't matter if it's water or it's wine.

The Sinner Prays for Permission

In the dark, she prays—*Father,*
I like to believe my delight

delights you, however
it arrives. But you are not

outwitted by desire; you
listen while I plait words

into strands thick enough to catch
fire. You, there to restrain me when

the hot glow of want leaves its red welt
on my cheeks, too close to the hunger

to turn away. *Once, just once … in this flesh,*
she bargains, asking anyway   any way.

You know how the body quickens, how breath
catches like a match, lit. You had a body once,

how you must have loved the rough crusts
in your hands, the flake of the silver-skinned fish

in your mortal mouth. Can I sway you, remembering
the fall of her hair, how it too held the sun?

Circuit

I quiver in bed-dark, heart chasing itself,
ringed like a caged bird or a captive, netted

and baited and bound. But the heart is just
a muscle that forces floods to flow in channels, into

filaments circling through tissue that is mainly meat
and bone and bright blood.

                    He's a prism, splitting day–
light into blue-flame, and all I think of is surrendering

to what carries us away, this hot exhale of air that bears us
between flat mud and flared stars. And how we orbit their fires,

clutched close in earth's dun fist, longing to burn.

Heat Lightning

These aren't the right conditions for a spark,
so what's electric, between midnight clouds,
just pulses bright and harmless in the heat.

The thunder closes in and rings us round.
There's nothing to be done but turn and praise
the hotly flickering display, nothing

we could be allowed to say. Sometimes the
sky can't bend and touch the earth, sometimes the
earth can't gather in the sky. They orbit

but they rarely intersect. Above are
other lights, less brilliant, steadier, dim
stars beyond this canopy of cloud. But

I do not cherish how I charted them,
a traveler now willingly off course.
The only lights I carry to my bed

are those now flaring in your silent eyes.

Ascension

All that summer I was climbing stairs. On the steep
hill from tram stop, I often took them two at once.

Other nights I wavered down the steps and wound
my way around the alleys to my heat-thick room.

One night he trailed me up those five full flights. We woke
to Sunday morning. Alone I scaled the curving streets,

past music shops and *lahmacun*, to church. I sat in one hard
pew and tried to pray. I took the bread and wine. I watched

the cross, that ladder strung between my heart and yours. I did
not want to climb it, wished you'd just come down. Quit dying

for these sins I could not manage to regret. Wished your pathway just
not quite so narrow, wished I could carry him across it on my own.

Felix Culpa

When I feel guilty for remembering you
so fondly, erasing your sharp edges, softening—
the way when I was young I liked snuffing out
a match-lit paper's corners that instant
just before they bloomed to flame—

then I remind myself you don't now recall my face, or
our two summers in that ancient, throbbing city.
Or how we drank too many satsuma cocktails
and you missed your ferry home. And how that night
I caught my own reflection in the bedroom mirror
and told her in a whisper that *you have the life you want.*

And when I think of seeing you again, I know that
what I really want is not the city or satsumas or bridge
lights pooling on the water, or the smell of fish and
sooty charcoal fires warming hazelnuts, the blood
in my chest at full flood, or the distant sound
of tea spoons singing against glass. Or even you,

pushing your way through my doorway. But want
again that certainty, the look in the face of the girl,
who spoke to the mirror and knew
her happiness, so long it had seemed from arrival.
Wish my body might remember its falling
through sea-salted air, into a radiant, swelling grace.

What Was Devoured

after Neruda's "El Tigre"

You do not even know what kind of animal I am.
You remember the waiting,
heavy as wet leaves,
but cannot describe my face.

The river ran like ink twisting
through underbrush. I led you.

I cloaked myself under innocence.
You were easy.

Then, I lay down
and fed my brief form
into your teeth, let you rip
what you thought was essential to desire
from my thin haunches.

You were ravenous. I wanted
devouring, piece by piece.

Now you keep watch
over the impotent bones
of your passion, years of rain
dampening your relentless
tales of conquest. But the creature
who lays herself down
outlasts her destruction.
What you name as love
was just power, disarmed
by surrender.

Cardiology

The heart does not relinquish
what it sometimes should. Clenches
in its bloody fist some ghost sensation.
Carries in a useless circle little pulses
that for years lay dormant, until some errant
fibrillating memory, a waft or wine-sip
brings you back and thumps arrhythmic,
through a synapse ribbon-tape that spells
a pattern in your name.
                              Ablation's what
they call it when they starve these wayward
circuits of their strength, and sever paths from
a tangled heart's electric line. To sever you
would be a wise oblation. But even if
I should, I would not will it.

Iconography

I would cover you with tin: stamped
milagros of flame, hearts, and arms,

whichever part needs touching most.
And hang you with glass bulbs—

a censer's earth-damp reliquary, scent
of magnolia—a hermitage. You become

a chapel I kneel inside, mouth open: waiting
for whatever grace is laid upon my tongue.

The Cathedral

It's what Rodin titled it that
draws the eye again. Two hands
cupped toward one another, knuckles
curving in to tenderly carve out a space in
air, the way a roofline mimics palms at prayer.

Is cathedral what he called this skeleton of bone,
that architects would call its joists and ribs?
Or is it what the shape of hands defines?
An emptiness that's known
by what it weighs.

Desideratum

Reflected light
is bright
but cold.

When it slices
through, the cut
is clean.

It won't take long
for blood to stitch
it up.

I wish that I could
find a way
to love with

   out

my body,

like angels
or how sunlight
loves what's green,

bringing it into being
and taking
nothing for itself.

On the Ferry

What I remember is, we were on water
       suspended in afternoon air on our way elsewhere
           but not having arrived.
What I remember is, sun scorching the surface
     'til the strait was a brilliant blue fire, and
         the soft canter of the boat beneath the gulls' white laughter.
We watched them gathering fish in the sparkling churn.
      I watched her, another passenger, her ankles crossed with her sister's,
         her veil smooth over dark brown hair, her eyes deeply
         awake   awake   awake.
The boat moved over water
    and slowly the shorelines dissolved
           between wherever it was we had come from
           wherever it was we went.
Belief spilled off me like water,
    the way a strand of hair strays from a forehead
       tender   thin   gone.
There was no more lake of fire.
    I could no longer make my heart fear
       in the way I'd been taught to fear.
The boat rowed us over
    the water, sun sparking in lengthening rays
       till the long wooden planks were extended.
I gathered my things for departure,
    pulled everything close as I crossed
       to the solid bank.
Sometimes now the sensation will flutter
    and I'll reach for my bags, an impulse of travelers,
       always reaching for what's been left behind.

The Denial of Saint Peter

Caravaggio, 1610

How could I leave?
All my stories are here
        —and you.

We stand around
like servant girls beside a fire
accusing ourselves—

       weren't we with him?
Our faces bright in light of
all that we keep circling,

a heat that gathers moths
as surely as it burns
away their wings.

A Swim

The desire is to dive down,
slip under the surface,
slide effortlessly through blue—

to let go of breath in all
its regular insistence,
the heart's demands—

to see beneath, a milky
light arresting altered eyes,
liquid dissolving distances

between what's concealed
and visible. The flesh
permits departure

not escape. The body
quieted, not shed. Arms
propel, limbs animate,

their rhythm patterning
our daily breath,
while we swim

in substances we barely see,
through and into, but
            not beyond.

III.

To a Friend, Lonely in the Fall

In fall at least the world doesn't lie to you
about dying, might even convince you you can
do it beautifully, become the blaze maple
transcendent against blue. The stands

of cottonwood that in summer appeared to be one
tree, unclasp green hands, separate and shiver
bare, remember they're alone. The light that angles
through the gold is not the kind that fills

the wanting in your core. Still, it can be caught
with words arranged on lines, like bait on hooks,
and fed upon. Because love is not a fullness, it's an
ache. Because one God I've known has loved me most

when He took everything away. The stark tree stripped
knows every name the wind goes by.

Nursling

after Psalm 131

When did I ever thirst as much?
Bend my body, thrash unwieldy
legs, wheel my arms to rock
toward a yielding warmth,
toward skin and gathering and milk?

Did I tune my ears to silence
when the singing stopped? My
newborn eyes still colorless
and dim, hungry for returning light.

No. I remember crying in the dark,
wandering empty hallways toward
my mother's room, trying
every door, my body weaned
off starlight now for good.

Chimayo

No one does kitsch as well as Catholics. Here, garish glass Madonnas
cradle red and yellow beams, the cloister lined by hand-strung
rosaries, walls crawling hives of glinting charms.

They close the church at service time. Bells spill their silver
ringing through the valley, reverberate off red rock hills, disturbing
red-winged blackbirds pinned on reeds of grass.

The air feels thin, as all the prayers said here have worn
a bare spot in earth's carpet. I peer at inverse worlds in clay,
walk on solid ground, but feel it ripple when I speak.

I come without need. Without crutches, bandages, or wounds.
Every bit the rich, the ones who Mary sang of, filled
in this life, empty in the next.

Others take their turns in *el pocito*, the little well of dirt
where they smear holy dust on palms and chests and feet.
I wait and count milagros in the nave.

The chapel's small, with crooked beams, floor sloping toward
the outside wall. I walk with measured steps like someone
on a heaving ship. The space holds still, air thick and undisturbed.

I mouth some hasty low-church prayer before I feel it, the emptiness
I share with history's women—the Rachels, the Elizabeths and Hannahs—
the infertile   the childless   the barren.

But I have little to complain of—my firstborn's almost three. I'm enduring
all the hormones, weekly probes, the daily charts, and little cups
of urine. But already I'm bone weary. I bend

and dab some red dirt on my fingers, smear it lightly on my empty
gut and swear, this will be the final cycle with the pills, before
I'll settle for my only son and let him be enough.

I do not bargain, plead or wail.
I ask, then brush the dirt from one hand to the next,
and duck my head beneath the low crossed beams to leave.

There's a poem that tells the moment Christ's small body first takes root
in a crevice of God's mind, depicted in mosaic on some Serbian church wall.
Mary forms in square-tiled glass, inside her, Christ the embryo, a single pane.

I suppose it's possible this might have been like that. The egg that since became
you stilled and waiting, lodged like a berry in the mouth of a blackbird, caught
like a seed in my prayerless throat.

Ultramarine

Even now, she's wearing her blue robe. On adobe
walls of missions, fixed to dashboards, cast as plaster
statuary, and in our childhood nativity the Made-
In-China figurine wears Mary-blue—a color,
I was told, reserved for virgins, but I doubt
she really wore it. That unearthly
shade of ultra-marine just a fiction
painters in the Middle Ages made by crushing
lapis and fermented minerals mined from
Silk Road destinations. A hue they use to drape
aristocrats and queens, the satisfied ones
she sang of, saying they would be sent away empty.

Trying to Conceive

Last month the test was negative and another you did not cohere.
They measured blood in little vials, gave me pills to make
the bleeding come or go and every day, I dipped a
sticky slip of paper in a little cup. They laid me
out on tables, peering in to see if you were
there. But you were not. There was not
even a you to not be, so nothing
has been lost at all. Just time.

It's hard to conceive how things might be
if you were. My belly growing taut and thick,
my mind arranging space for you in ordered lives,
and how we'd decorate, dust off the bassinette. But every
month's an otherwise, each possible eludes us, swept off like
seedlings washed downhill by rain. This, the nature of things. What
finally comes to being comes with shadows, carries with it all the absences
that rest in everything.

What the Mother Says on Birthdays

We had looked for you for days, for weeks, the probe
between my thighs by then a practiced pinch.

Before you were a twinkle—
that's the saying, but should better be

before you were a sliver in your mother's
side, a hiccup, or a sting. I saw you,

pebble on the monitor, my neck lifting
off the sterile pillow, to tilt toward the TV

—your brother entertained by goldfish
crackers in his stroller tray beside me.

Trans-vaginal made me think of trans-Siberian, some
wilderness of train tracks, wind whipping over barren

wastes. Or of trans-Atlantic, the swollen silver bellies
of the planes glinting off the surface of the sea. You

journeyed toward us slowly—at least, the half of you I held.
It was like peering in the brain to watch a thought at its

inception, a poem struggling for form before its words.
Maybe I had wanted just to keep you to myself, the way

some memories are kept beautiful unsaid. I held you longer
than I should, when all the body asked of me—*release.*

Latch

What they don't remind you
is that *milk* can be a verb,
the specialists who come to tilt
the baby to your breast.

Your lost modesty surprises as
you wrestle with a nipple toward
the socket of his mouth.
Your audience assesses

every latch, the rounding of his lips
against the milk-white of your chest.
For now, you are his everything. A
symbiosis forms between supply

and his demand, the most primal
of economies. What they don't
discuss is that *milk* is still
a verb, and you're its object.

Night Shift

Night is a mouth,
hungry and endless
in its demands.

You offer your body,
its brief power
to soothe and quiet.

Sometimes you're enough.
Through sleeplessness
you tell yourself

this is the easy part.
Be grateful for the pangs
that are quieted by milk,

the hungers that respond
to flesh. Holding him,
you know there will be nights,

like yours, when nothing will
satisfy, that an open mouth
can wait forever to be filled.

The Interior of Oude Kerk, Amsterdam

Emmanuel de Witte, 1660

In the corner, doused in light that spills
over her bundled hair and shoulders, and the basket
holding round loaves wrapped in linen, she nurses a child
who looks old enough to walk, and another waits in shadows
with a mangy dog. Who knows if this is the painter's plain
Madonna, the middle-class Dutch version of divinity?
She is not robed in color on the walls. Her sturdy arms and legs
have been lifting milk-jugs and the children, and wrestling
with that dog for kitchen scraps. And I can tell you
she is tired, tired in the marrow of her bones, too tired
to tarry here much longer modeling the Holy Mother
with this homespun basket of Eucharistic bread.
The baby's crying and no doubt there are meals to make
beyond the one that's made of her own body. I can hear her
scolding the painter as she sits, her head spinning
with all the rough chores that stand between her and
the moment she lies down on her bed at last, unwraps
her hair from its linen halo and finally sleeps.

Taking the Baby to See Rothko
at the National Gallery

Fifteen minutes before closing seems like more time than we'll need to see all there is to see in Rothko's blocks of color, the hungry purples gnawing on their canvases, the primal reds. The baby likes the moving walkway, mobiles, flickering lights, the blueberry rooster crowing at the city from the roof. I assume abstract expressionists will be a bit beyond his comprehension, forgetting that they're art stripped down to form, to rectangle and red, to line and lack.

But when his eager babbles echo off the surfaces in Rothko's room, I see he understands it more than I do, pre-verbal, full of awe, himself another masterpiece of bright, unsayable things.

Bath Time

My son cups his hands beneath the faucet
laughing. Clear water rushes in
to fill the bath. Sun floods
the angled windows and parts his hair

in thin white ribbons. His eyes
widen, catching a glimpse
of their own brightness
in the metal disk of the drain.

His fingers stretch and wiggle, trying
to grasp the rivers, keep them
from spilling out of his tiny palms. I
look at him and see the years ahead

when everything he tries to hold
will slip away.
The tub fills and rippling echoes
off the hard walls while I kneel,

turn the knob and stop the flow.
But not before I run my own hands
in the stream, curving mine
beneath his as he laughs.

Learning again from him how to want
to gather everything,
and the play the water makes
as we let it go.

Midlife Valentine

You will not believe me when I tell you there are years
you will want nothing more than sleep and to be kissed
senseless by the quiet.

There were other years you thought you needed beauty
the way the girls in fairy tales need magic rings, or locks
of hair, or golden coins. A talking bird, a shoe.

You will not believe me when I tell you it's the wanting
that you'll miss the most, once your lap is full of everything
you thought you'd go without.

Those years you made a compass of desire, the way
you make a paper heart by folding it in half,
and cutting what is left of it away.

Clipping

My own words have
forsaken me. I nest

in others for awhile,
or gather scraps of

sound that flew from
my own throat when

my wings were a
different color and not

yet tame.

Trying to Get My Body Back

As if the baby had slithered away with it. As if I had carried a spare
change of bodies into the hospital in my overnight bag. As if a trapper had
come in the night, slit it from me like a pelt, leaving me pooled
in the bedsheets. As if I were a game
show and svelte models displayed my body on a turntable, glittering
in the Showcase Showdown. As if my body had run off to join the circus, wanted
to be the girl who is shot from a canon. As if it had wagered itself on a hand
of poker and lost to a man with diamond teeth. As if it were a nautilus, emptied
on the beach. As if it were a shopping cart, a locker key, a rented suit. As if
I had pawned my body for cash.

But not as if the body can't empty and fill, empty and fill, like a harbor.
Not as if lungs don't give birth to breath, pregnant again every pause.
As if it can't grow like a sea star, relimbing itself from a center.
Or that the body might think it's a wardrobe, larger inside than out,
might fold itself in like tent, or dissolve
like an old country's borders—a crossing shuttered, the guards asleep.
Not as if bodies can't winter like gardens, or ebb like a river.
As if my body hadn't borne me itself. Had wanted to be a cathedral
sounded, or a chamber echoed, a canyon hollowed
by waters—all fullnesses formed by what has been sculpted away.

Desert Parable

A dragonfly kites to the corner of the room,
its body a silver pin, tissue wings a desert's vellum,
a parchment scribed with the short story of rain.

High desert's stucco emptiness is mapped
by bare arroyo, arid canyon. A nothing writ
with piñon, yucca, succulents, by crows

aloft on updrafts, tattooing themselves on clouds.
Brief rain arrives to succor brittle bark, demands,
do much with little, as one leaf with its gathered light.

What Bears the Light

What bears light best is broken—
sea-glass sand-scattered,
mica fleck-pressed into stone,

tessera tile bits glinting under plaster.
The shattered mirror throws a thousand
faces through the air.

What bears best is broken—
light spills, splinters, wanders
through wave-crest, in ripple-riven

surfaces of lakes disturbed by wind.
What bears best is broken—
the heart, broken. The bread.

The robin-blue shell and the crocus bulb
bear beauties, and every spring renew
their breaking open

IV.

To the Women Marching, from a Mother at Home

It is cold, and my son is small.
I rock him in the fragile boat of my body
between this night's dark and a brighter shore.

We are always awake.

He curves at my breast like a comma
between the words anchored deep in my chest,
and the breath taking form in his lungs.

In the quiet, we hear your chanting.

Remember us with you, we are the rear-guard.
I am carrying him like a banner, feel him
cutting his teeth on my curdled milk.

I am sharpening him like an arrow.

Pablo C. Tiersten, 38, Kansas City

Authorities found a man shot dead inside a home
after four long hours standoff with police.

News print's the first small box the dead are made
to lie in. The marshals pulled you from a closet,

a fugitive slipping past them in the end. You died
in Kansas City, but called the City of Angels home.

Whether life allowed you tenderness or not, I only guess.
But when I birthed a son, they pulled him out, I drew him

close, and every minute since have held a searing image
of his crumpled body—an accident—a fall—or mangled

by a car, some lapse of my attention. I carry an expectant
grief. I believe when your end came, *Pablo*, your eyes

were open in that darkness. Though you must not have heard
the city's angels singing, as they always do, *be not afraid.*

And afterwards, I made you this small song to sing against this
country's violent dark— an inadequate display of grief's attention.

Yesterday you still moved under our common sky. Today I found
your year's old photo of the Virgin Mother, and your capslock praise

of *LOVE HER.* She will shroud you now in deep blue robes, your body
laid across her lap. For just this very moment, you're her only son.

Revised Common Liturgy

For the National Day of Prayer

What is the invocation of the immigration lawyer,
asleep on the airport floor? The collect
of the pedestrian-clogged capital, the rite
of the nationwide boycott, the litany for pussy

hats, safety pins, sign-up sheets? What's the intercession
against pornstar payoffs and pepper spray? Are protests
thumbed on touchscreens antiphons?

Tweet.
Retweet.
And also with you.

What is the prayer made by the door you didn't slam
at your parent's house on Christmas Day, the throat-lump
swallowed down with pie? The tongue bitten
was a prayer. The tongue held.

Pray anger.
Pray bile.
Pray blisters.

We are learning to make the sign
of crossing the diner to muzzle the rifle
that burns our dark hands.

We are learning to make the signs
out of poster board,

because
we have not loved our neighbors
as ourselves. We have not loved.
We have not.

The thorns on the roses in the Garden, too, are prayers.

Upon Seeing a Photograph of Christine Blasey Ford

I think first of Joan of Arc—that movie version where
her hair's shorn, her pained gaze skyward as the flames
lick the edges of the frame. Next I think of Magdalene
running from the garden, her body brimming
with the unbelievable, becoming not the last woman
whose story's just a little too convenient, whose
reputation's made to be dismissed. These allusions are
intentional, I know, the photographer has framed her,
elevated from his vantage with that upraised arm,
and no one else in view.
       Every day we're desperate for icons worthy of
our prayers. Her steady rendering of memory reminds me
no ordinary woman ever tried to be a saint. Who would
choose to be believed in when she'd rather be believed?

Gallery

if you aren't happy   no one can tell
here is the place to imagine

what it might be like to be adored
gather glass smooth as stone   mineraled rare

earth   pixel stitches   certain angles
of bone   foreheads unworried as angels

what is it again that women are loved for?   all this
time and I still don't know   perfection

makes me want to show you the tear   in my dress
in my belly   my adornments of shrapnel

try it on   the gaze   that calculates
it's clear-eyed   like water in the bucket

where they shuck pearls   out of their shells
bare   ly   a shimmer worth wearing

the nacre wound   a mirage
where what remains   unkempt

Monologue of the Juno Probe

They have named me for a woman
who could pull the curtains back and peer
at the ineffable by inches.
I have one eye and broad wings for catching sun
and instructions to approach the god
slantwise to his poles.
Truth is come to by peregrinations
then a scurry to safety, flame faced and bright,
like Moses on the mountain glimpsing backside
of the Holy, like the woman grasping Jesus' robe
and slipping through the crowd
possessed of power and changed.
Perijove by perijove I dive into the clouds
and show you how they eddy,
how Jupiter's a turbulence of fire, how
we learn to circle toward a power
we cannot not describe or tether,
an orbit around what governs us
but we cannot touch. If we're careful
we can glimpse it
looking backwards as we go.

Inherit the Earth

"We believe in changing hearts first," my mother says
to the canvasser who knocked for Save the Whales. The eighties:
humpbacks are the cause célèbre. We know this from the episode
where Captain Kirk woos the Lady Scientist, quotes DH Lawrence,
 "they say the sea is cold, but the sea contains the hottest blood of all"

—the whales save us, the Enterprise flies forward in space-
time to a better world that's just this one technicolored free
of radiation, racism, money or religion. Sci-Fi's promises
are beguiling as salvation, and we understand that impulse,
singing Sundays *I'll fly away, oh glory, I'll fly away.*

I wish my mom had said, "We can't afford to give"—but hearts
are all that last. Why waste your money saving what will burn?
Faith's fires demand you get yourself out first, and only if
there's time turn back and hose the house that's going up in flames.
This world is not my home, I'm just a-passin through.

But now at night my son and I look up. He asks about the universe,
spun galaxies, all those nameless moons with singeing rains. We've
seen the signs of planets around distant stars in habitable zones
—that narrow band where water can exist as liquid, not as vapor
or as ice. We detect these worlds by wobbles in their stars.

My son's warm body curves toward mine as I tally up cold spheres
of rock and gas: no life, no life. There is no other life we've ever found.
It would take a dozen years for a message to reach Luyten's star and,
if it were received by something there, another dozen for an answer
to come back. After that we read about blue whales singing low,

calling through the oceans for each other. My son drifts off to sleep
while pages name and number systems, brilliant glossy blossoms, star-
warmed worlds pulsed by possibility. But I don't want him dreaming
of Kirk's technicolored world, I wish him grasp the rare blue-green
impossibility of ours.

Our Lady of the Ruins

Somewhere along the line   we learned   not to run   like horses
from   the flames   that salvation comes   by standing   in
one place   and passing   pieces   hand   to   hand   Yours is
the corner chapel   I keep lit   where I keep   coming
back   to sweep   the worn stone   smooth   The crossbeams
crumble   under fire and leave us   staring at the black
hole   they   concealed   but which was always there
fringed now by the flames   The bees   we've not
extinguished yet   have taken   to drinking   tears
These stones are   only ever just   the frame we shape
around   what cannot   be   escaped   the way a telescope
collects   the dark   Our last lyric is   The fire's tongue
that whispers   Come   there's always more   to lose
And maybe   this time   Christ   the bee   survives
knitting   a salty honey   from the iris dark

Walburga Catechism

The wind breathes hot on tumbles of red stone.
Dust exhales behind the combing plow, hay parts
in crescent rows. Paint on cross-beams peels
and cactus flowers wither in the wheat.

> *Why would the Word take on such heat-flushed flesh?*
> *So thus we might know love.*

I bend to pick up chunks of granite stone
and place them on each Station's cracking limb,
where moths cocoon in figures of reliefs,
white floss wraps linen shrouds across the beams.

> *How is it that the Son of God is man?*
> *St. Teresa said, Christ has no body but your own.*

So whose feet press this ground, and smooth the scorched
moss on the sun-turned bellies of the rocks?
Grasshoppers green at ankles, watching sisters
in their habits the same color as this sky.

> *How in wilderness can we speak the names of God?*
> *We can name God only by taking creatures as our starting point.*

So something unknown names itself in wind
that prays through windows of the church, the space
between the panes an open throat voicing
mercy in a high-pitched tongue, and I think
how misery and mercy sound the same.

Why did the Word take on flesh?
Christ's body was finite, therefore the human face of Christ can be portrayed.

When I was young, I remember hearing
of the crucifix, We should not glory
in his death, He's no longer on that cross.
No, I think, but we are. I want to smooth
his broken body in my hands and mouth
the sound of mercy like a round stone.

This place, this native ground of weeping, this
stretched blue and this bristled sage unhallowed
by history or name, but still angels
pass between red-tumbles of the boulders,
as new and bright arrivals to this air.

This is the only place where I can learn
to love, the only body given me
to wear. I carry it by habit through
this sky and try on every color's name.
Caught up in love of things invisible,
known only by resemblance to what's seen.

Whose Streams

after Psalm 46

So tell me the name of that river, and how
I might drown. After long distance, I learned

I should take off my boots,
tie the laces together, sling them

over my pack and wade through
the foam, sometimes circling

my ankles, sometimes knee-deep
while the pack-weight pressed my soles

to the mud, or I trembled, tottering slick
on the gem-bright rocks. Once across,

we sat on the boulders, rubbed
the grooves on our shins from ribbed socks,

dried our feet in the sun, ran
thumbs along tendons and returned

our swelled feet to stiff shoes.
Can I say this is gladness? How clear

water shimmers in memory, that once
you were carried along, that once

you knew enough to take off your shoes,
as you do at a threshold,

how you are stilled there in the torrent
while the river sings.

Wild Leaven, Taos

Doors open and bells ring, the saints
on walls wear cornflower sky,
and every tilted ladder promises a fall

through incalculable blue.
Light flaked down in the valley lodges
in the mica dust. The women tell me how

they make designs on pots
by wrapping horsehair through
the glittered clay, then burning

it away. The smudge remains
in soot-singed strands.
What am I trying to say?

That there's light
and what light passes through
to be detectable.

Wild leaven, unseen, borne through air,
can still be made a sustenance, like all things
nourishing if taken in.

I sift the dust and grind the mica
pebbles underneath the pestle of my feet.
I light the wick of marrow that I carry

with me everywhere, but cannot form
a prayer, just hold my heart
out like a bucket, like an unrung bell.

Love is realest in journeying,
indistinguishable from motion
transporting us between our destinations.

We pass a shrine along the road, carved
from rock and strung with beads, dotted
in daylight by faint lights behind glass.

If I would be a saint, let it be
the patron saint of prisms, a face
shaped for reflection. Be the body

breaking everything else open, one that splits
the burning day into its myriad beams.
Let me be passed through.

Acknowledgements

SOME POEMS IN THIS collection may have appeared in earlier versions in my two chapbooks *Visitations* (Finishing Line 2015) and *Latch* (River Glass 2019) and in the following journals & anthologies:

All We Can Hold: Poems of Motherhood. Sage Hill: "Bath Time"
America, We Call Your Name: Poems of Resistance & Resilience. Sixteen Rivers: "To the Women Marching, From a Mother at Home."
Amethyst Review: "On Being Asked If Share the Gospel with my Students," "On the Ferry," Perestroika"
Cagibi: "Heat Lightning," "Bodies of Water," "Cardiology," "Revised Common Liturgy"
Cherry Tree: "Our Lady of the Ruins"
The Christian Century: "Dualism for Beginners," "The Interior of Oude Kerk, Amsterdam," "At Hagia Irene," "Monologue of the Juno Probe"
The Cresset: "Desert Parable," "Detail of a Peacock"
Harpur Palate "Wild Leaven, Taos"
In A Strange Land: Introducing 10 Kingdom Poets. Poiema Poetry Series. Cascade: "Walburga Catechism"
Inklette: "Midlife Valentine"
Kanstellation: "Circuit"
Mom Egg Review: "Night Shift," "Taking the Baby to See Rothko at the National Gallery"
The Other Journal: "A Swim"
Poetry Birmingham: "Gallery"
The Priscilla Papers: "Jeanne D'Arc"
Relief Journal: "To the Guest Who Broke a Wine Glass at my Party"
Rock & Sling: "Nursling," "The Sinner Prays for Permission," "Iconography"
Ruminate: "Trying to Conceive," "Trying to Get My Body Back"
Rust & Moth: "To a Friend Lonely in the Fall"
St. Katherine Review: "Ash Wednesday"
Sky Island Review: "Desideratum"
Spoon River Poetry Review: "Upon Seeing a Photograph of Christine Blasey Ford," "What Was Devoured"
Structo: "Whose Streams"
Whale Road Review: "What the Mother Says on Birthdays"
The Windhover: "Ascension," "Ultramarine," "The Cathedral"

I am grateful to the publications listed who have honored my poems in the following ways:

"Jeanne D' Arc" and "Renunciation" in *The Priscilla Papers* earned 4th place for Poetry at the Evangelical Press Association for publication year 2008. "Bodies of Water" in *Cagibi* was nominated for a 2019 "Best of the Net" award. "Trying to Conceive," and "Trying to Get My Body Back" were each finalists for *Ruminate Magazine's* McCabe Poetry prize in 2017 and 2018, respectively. "To the Women Marching, from a Mother at Home," was nominated for a Pushcart Prize by *Sixteen Rivers Press* in 2018. "Upon Seeing a Photograph of Christine Blasey Ford," was selected as a runner up for the 2019 *Wolverine Farm Press* Poetry Broadside Prize. "Whose Streams," was the winner of *Structo Magazine's* 2019 Psalm Translation contest.

I also wish to thank a number of editors whose encouragement and attention have been vital to my growth as a writer. Specific thanks go to the presses which produced my two chapbooks, some of the contents of which have found their way into this book. Thank you to Leah Maines and the staff at Finishing Line Press for their work on "Visitations" (2015). A warm thank you as well goes to Marley and Kimberly Dawn Stuart at River Glass Books who were a joy to work with on "Latch" (2019). I am grateful for Jeffery Levine and Kirsten Miles at Tupelo Press and for the Tupelo 30/30 Project community of writers. Thanks also to D.S. Martin for his belief in my work, his patient shepherding of this project, and his selection of a number of my poems for the recent Cascade Books anthology, "In a Strange Land: Introducing Ten Kingdom Poets."

I owe immeasurable thanks to the fellow writers & artists whose insights, collaboration, feedback and friendship have enriched my writing and my life. Deepest thanks to Katie Manning, Sally Rosen Kindred, Tania Runyan, Matthew Landrum, Christine Darragh, Elizabeth Dark, Nelle Smith, Kristin Marshall, Natalie Collins, Cameron Lawrence and David Harrity.

I owe a tremendous debt of gratitude to those who have helped me care for my two young sons while their mama was writing: Ivy Garcia, Aunt Krissy Spaeth, Nana & Papa Stewart, and Grammie & Poppy Fueston.

Lastly, to John. I couldn't have done this without your steady care and support. For all we've created and continue to create together, I am grateful.

Notes on the poems

"Tekakwitha" takes its name from the first indigenous American saint, Kateri Tekakwitha, a 17th century Algonquin-Mohawk woman, who was canonized by the Catholic Church in 2012.

"Hagia Irene" means "Holy Peace," and is the name of the Byzantine-era church which hosted the 1st Council of Constantinople in 381 A.D, which sought to clarify the doctrine of the divinity of the Holy Spirit.

In "The Virgin, Home from the Mall," the annunciation painting referred to is Dante Rossetti's "Ecce Ancilla Domini," in which he used his sister, the poet Christina Rossetti, as a model for the Virgin Mary.

"Felix Culpa" refers to the theological concept of the "fortunate fall"—the idea that The Fall creates the possibility of redemption through the work & revelation of Christ.

"To a Friend, Lonely in the Fall" is for Matthew Landrum.

"The Denial of St. Peter" is for David Harrity.

"Chimayo" is a pilgrimage site in northern New Mexico, El Santuario de Chimayo, where many visitors are reported to have experienced healing. The poem referenced in the penultimate stanza is Jane Kenyon's "Mosaic of the Nativity, Serbia, Winter 1993."

"Trying to Get My Body Back" is for Katie Manning.

"Pablo C. Tiersten, 38, Kansas City" was written for the 2015 Lament for the Dead project, which aimed at drawing attention to incidents of violence between police and US citizens. Each day, a volunteer poet received information about an individual who had died the previous day—both officers and citizens—and wrote an elegy on behalf of that person.

"Monologue of the Juno Probe" comes from NASA's ongoing Juno mission to gather data from beneath the planet's top layer of gaseous cloud. In Roman mythology, the god Jupiter draws a veil around himself to hide his mischief (correspondingly, the moons of Jupiter are named after mythological lovers and offspring), and his wife, the goddess Juno, is able to peer behind the curtain to reveal his true nature.

"Walburga Cathechism" takes its name from the Abbey of St. Walburga, a small community of contemplative Benedictine nuns who live and work in an isolated rural area of Northern Colorado.

www.ingramcontent.com/pod-product-compliance
Lightning Source LLC
LaVergne TN
LVHW041305080426
835510LV00009B/870